AMERICAN TALES

NEESHANT SRIVASTAVA

For the angels in my life.

Contents

My Country 'tis of Thee   *vii*

1. SPINDLE IN AMERICA   1

2. LAZY NIGHTS WITH BEER   4

3. SPINDLE THE ROGUE   8

4. THE GAMBLING SPREE   12

5. SPINDLE AND THE DUMPSTER   17

6. THE STORE   20

7. SPINDLE AND NIGHT SHIFTS   23

8. DEEP CUT BELOW THE PINKY FINGER   26

9. SABOBA CASINO   29

10. THE SIX FLAGS TRIP   32

11. THE SECOND QUARTER   37

12. THE THIRD SEASON   43

13. RIDE TO LA   47

14. MRS. TURNER AT THE STORE   50

15. THE FAT LADY   52

16. THE FINAL SEE OFF   55

My Country 'tis Of Thee

Sweet land of Liberty

MY COUNTRY 'TIS OF THEE

ONE

SPINDLE IN AMERICA

A black Indian boy in America is quite an unusual thing, especially if he is born in the remote state of Bihar, India. Bihar with its lost glory is perhaps the worst place to live in India. Here people don't live, they die every day because of malnutrition, dearth of jobs, unhygienic environment and the poor dumped in bed less government hospitals. Still, we churn out the best brains in the world and America is sweet to cling to like horseflies.

Spindle had no brains. You can most politely ask him to do away with the garbage or you can ask him to scrub the floor, or maybe tickle your earlobes, he will do it with finesse. When his old father one day asked Spindle to go to America, he just shook his head the Indian way. He somehow landed in the American Consulate with a group of ten greedy Delhi boys for group visa to fly away to America.

Spindle was not happy,

"Papa after all these years of my serving you and listening to you and loving you, why in the world are you throwing me away to a distant land."

Papa was not amused and thought silently,

"Stupid bugger, don't you even know why young people go to America? Just to have some fun, silly. And what about those girls, baby. You can easily catch one of them and go for a little ride. C'mon you are big enough for me to explain such things to you. Besides the white love the black and baby some hot girl might just have hots for you. After all you are six feet tall, honey."

"Papa, you have screwed my life, I hate you."

Spindle was asleep on the flight that had a stopover at Seoul, South Korea for four hours. Each student was supposed to get on the kiosk and send emails to loved ones that they had made it half way and LA was not a distant dream now. Spindle lazily zapped one email to his brother but somewhere he lacked enthusiasm. On the flight his Punjabi friend drank his quota of four beers and then nudged Spindle to expend his own quote for a sweet guzzle. Spindle obliged, like always and beer to him was like fish oil, so horrible and 'yuck'. The plane took off to the skies and at about thirty thousand feet, it was docked as if it were not moving at all and the guest were served boiled vegetables in the Korean airline. Spindle just returned the thing wrapped which he thought was most rude. But Spindle could not help it.

After a drama of many hours hanging in the air the plane finally touched down on the great LA International Airport. Spindle had heard a song on LA International Airport,

"*Where the big jet engine rolled...*"

There was nothing glamorous about the airport and the taxing lasted for about three hours until the seat hurt to the extent of rolling big thighs to the left and right on the seat to make it little bearable while children with not such heavy baggage had fun. The plane just moved and moved on the runway as if the sun would knock overheard at noon very soon, touching down at exactly 5:45 AM.

Ten Delhi boys were taken in a typical stylish American van to Guesthouse Inns and Suites, Santa Ana, California.

Then came an angel by the name of Ms. Carmel Cruz. I believe that there is a clan of people than love Mark Knopfler music or a Paul Simon special and it takes a lifetime or nothing to get there. Carmel Cruz was mentioned by Spindle's father as someone that he must first meet, besides a wholesale brother. Spindle walked into the lobby to the reception very gingerly. There stood a lady with rosy cheeks, white complexion and a happy disposition.

"Could I have your autograph please."

"Excuse me, are you referring to me."

"Yes, of course, please don't delay, I have stuff to take care of."

"Why, sure, if I only knew why."

"You will, one day, honey."

"Excuse me, was that 'honey'"

Spindle was confused like clouds on a sunny day. But the air was very clean and vision was greatly enhanced by the clean air. Spindle felt the pure air in his lungs and was quite surprised to see not enough trees and birds. The grass was perfectly trimmed and a perfect cushion for costly shoes that could never get dirty. People here got allergic to something as subtle as pollen from flowers on the trees. There was not enough people in America and the empty spaces were sometimes too scary and loneliness could easily spoil a prefect day with blue skies, green grass, clean air and golden sunshine. Ten boys from Delhi joined ten boys from Mumbai. Like all around the world, especially in America where beauty is no taboo and woman hardly have much on their bodies by way of clothes, men from third world countries dream of such heaven. Twenty-four hours Delhi and Mumbai boys talked of nothing but sex with those blond beauties, although indirectly and in a great hush trying to appear noble like some sadhu or hermit. Spindle too dreamt of such an encounter but perhaps lacked the gumption and the guile to try to snatch one or try to engender a long affair ending in a great time in bed, although the girl would be flabbergasted for she would have desired it right on the first date.

Well, the boys created a great ruckus, and I shall continue with their adventures in my next story from the American tales.

TWO
LAZY NIGHTS WITH BEER

Spindle had some association with beer. Once as a fifteen-year-old he was to travel to Delhi with his father. The rest of the family did not matter for Spindle hardly remembered anyone around as a child except his father. Mother was always lost in her own world with her own 'friends' which included the sweeper Shanti, the maid Laxmi and the very old Baba 'kabariwala' Shambhu. Brother hardly uttered a word and had already entered deep meditation which later on gave him a ticket to posh places like Manhattan in the city of New York and admission in the Ivy league college, Columbia University. One has to be very lucky indeed to be at such places. Manhattan was something my father read in story books when he dreamt of going to sunny California as a young man. Places like San Franscisco and LA and what not were like drops of heaven and Champs-Élysées in Paris was where he sipped coffee in a coffee bar in his amazing dreams, poor baby.

Coming back to Spindle's rather dull and dreary trip to Delhi when back then Delhi had slowly turned into a hot smoking bowl. One could feel steam in the atmosphere when there was no sun to speak of, just a haze of black clouds. Spindle often tried to peek at the sun through his eyes and could only gather a very blurred outline of the sun. Well, that was back then, when Spindle was just

15 years old, in the year 1989. What has happened to Delhi, perhaps we all know and being the most polluted city in the world, perhaps not at the top of the list anyway is not surprising. What Spindle most regretted, even back then, was the language they use in Delhi, a kind of Hindi that has been adulterated and made putrid and ugly. Later in life Spindle did happen to go to Noida which is almost a second Delhi and the language used was most unbecoming of the 'Tehzeeb' in the 'lehja' that we Indians pride ourselves. Spindle believed that if you do not know how to speak to people in the correct manner in which you should address people, especially older people, then we haven't transcended fully into a complete human being. Come to a place like Patna or go to Rajasthan, you will find what 'respect' is. Delhi has become a place for those high collar rough guys that like to blast their motorbikes every afternoon on busy streets and carry a girlfriend in their pocket for fun.

Coming back to the beer tale, Spindle's father was hurrying for their trip to Delhi. Luggage was ready with hold-all and a huge family suitcase that had been with the family through thick and thin and like a guard always carried whatever rubbish they threw into it. Everything was in perfect readiness, Spindle's father in his kurta pyjama had to just jump into the shower and wear his immaculate dress of creased long trousers and full creased shirt and those shoes that just spoke volumes of the retired Air Force officer.

"Spindi, quick take a shower now, we have to rush. O! my God wait, honey. What have I done. There are three chilled bottles of beer in here. What am I going to do. I cannot drink all of it Spindi, I am about to travel. Can you help me please and drink all this stuff, quickly. You can do it Spindi, come."

"Papa, how can I drink all of it. And I don't like it anyways, I had secretly tried it once when we had a party at our home last week, Papa. It's horrible Papa, I don't like it."

"You are right baby, it is not good after all, I hear 'ya."

"Let's then throw it all away somewhere, I guess the ants shall have a party somewhere. You please get ready, we should not waste any more time, honey."

This was Spindle's 'beer' history. Spindle had tasted it alright, but he detested it strongly to this day.

Boys are boys as they say and at some point of time in their lives, they turn into adults just by the size of their chest and when the unspeakable, quite popular among women, becomes huge. Just then one needs to guzzle pints of beer and quickly lose virginity with some hot girl, well the girls love it anyways. The boys once decided to have a beer party. The hotel staff had their eyes on the boys and were expecting things to go slightly out of hand. Indians are milder than their American friends and they say that one should never mess around with white Americans and if happens to be a woman, then may God be by your side. Spindle too happened to join the boys for beer. They first gave him a tall can of the local beer and asked him to drag it into his throat. It was just about 11:30 PM when the great deliberation began. Twenty or so years are enough for maturity and beer is just a bitter pill that men consume to prove to the women, especially, that they are goof enough to sizzle their nights. Love and the aftermath are a good thing, it is perhaps the most beautiful thing in this world, but when it gets adulterated with lust, which it does in most cases, then it gets rather ugly.

Spindle drank from the whole can which must have been about 800 ml, if memory serves him right, being alive enough to this day to talk about it. Don't ask Spindle how and when we should have lots of beer, empty stomach or full stomach. He just drank and felt nothing, just the stomach rumbling with 800 ml of beer and wondering what to do with it. Urine takes time and Spindle was offered a second can of the local beer that was rather chilled for him to finish it quickly. By that time the clock had struck 1:30 AM and the staff was all gone and the hotel attendant walked out and requested the boys to call it a day, it was unnecessarily disturbing other guests. They paid not heed and half way through the second can of the local beer, Spindle began to tire and his body rejected any further consumption. The boys were more drunk than tipsy as some of them had scotch whiskey. They pushed Spindle and like a fool he finished the second can with a huge burp. At this time the time was

2:30 AM and the boys were given stern warning to shove their asses onto their beds. Now Spindle was through with a third can of beer and rushed to the bathroom. He threw up on the bath tub and the boys just left his side with a slap of disgust on their foreheads and locked him in the bathroom.

THREE

SPINDLE THE ROGUE

Spindle travelled to America with a group of ten Delhi boys. The flight had taken off from New Delhi International airport. Papa had forcibly pushed Spindle to join this company that promised to send ten lads to California as a part of a twining program with UC Irvine, California. It was going to be a short four months certificate program in which the boys were to learn Embedded systems. Spindle had no clue about Embedded systems and all he could gather was that there was something 'embedded' somewhere that made these electronic devices, especially those marvellous computers work.

Spindle had a degree in Mechanical Engineering. It took him almost seven years to get the degree when in the usual course it takes just four years, all over the world. The college where he studied had late sessions when it normally took about six years to get the degree. Spindle happened to flunk in the second year, which meant he took seven years to graduate. The students of the college labelled the college as the 'worst' college in the world. Papa was not happy to see Spindle just sit and wait for some exam with was always postponed indefinitely. The reason for such an occurrence was that the teaching and the non-teaching staff did not get pay for years. It is a record that one professor had not gotten his pay for six years. The University to which the college was affiliated never gave any funds to the college because the higher brass robbed away all the money from the University treasury. In such a situation the dissatisfaction trickled down to the students who sat on an indefinite hunger strike quite often. They demanded exams, which is quite ridiculous, because students run away from any kind of test or exam. It got so frustrating for one student that he jumped off a running train and committed suicide. Spindle was quite patient in such a situation but his father wasn't,

"Baby, don't do this to me. Please walk out this place and take admission in some college of Architecture. I know you love drawing. There is still time, honey. I don't know when you will graduate. Sometimes you are beyond me, I tell you. You are very obstinate. Come let's have some 'bhuja', they prepare some nice concoction here."

Father would often be found walking in the college campus just to gee up Spindle and talk to the professors for some light somewhere,

"Mr. Srivastava, the train has come to a halt, try to understand. It will move someday. Look at me, these cigarettes are just not enough to bide away my time and I know I will die very soon."

When finally, after seven years of slogging Spindle finally graduated, Papa was really happy and proud.

"That's my boy. 57% overall, that amazing Kido. Now you are to rest and only rest. This IT field is really hotting up, I hear. Well son, you'll get to sit in an AC room all day and do magical things with these new things called computers. I know, if I let you go you will join hands with those blue-collar workers and spend the rest of your life repairing cars. Son, I want you to go to America and IT is a great and easy way to get there. Listen to me, don't play the dumb ass. Life is not a bed of roses, son."

Coming back to the company that Spindle joined that had a total of ten boys. All ten got the visa and that day Papa was over the moon. He actually laughed which was a rare sight and everyone around him were taken by surprise including Mom. Papa caught the evening train in some bogey and did not sleep all night in the train. He reached Spindle's lodge and hugged his son. He gave Spindle big cash and helped him pack his bags. Spindle was to take the 1:30 AM flight from New Delhi International airport to Seoul, as a layover, and then to California from there. Papa had a tear when he saw Spindle last, receding in the distance, until the wave of his hands died down and he headed back in great loneliness. It is said that Papa could not bear the loneliness and took his life one year later when Spindle was in America.

Spindle reached the hotel where they were to stay and had met Ms. Carmel Cruz as mentioned. He rushed to get a room with the Delhi boys. For some reason he was a tad late to approach the hotel for a room. He had been tied up with his brother. The Delhi boys blankly refused to offer a place to Spindle, saying that all rooms had been occupied. Spindle in disgust decided to leave the hotel known as the 'The Guesthouse Inns and Suites' and had no idea where to head next, neither did his brother. Just then an unfamiliar face approached him seeing Spindle in distress. This was a tall, lanky, white boy from Mumbai by the name of Animesh Shintre. He nudged Spindle,

"Hi, are you looking for a room. You can join me. I am one of the Mumbai boys. We are a group of ten and arrived here just at just about the same time as the Delhi boys."

Spindle was elated. He shook hands with Animesh,

"You can call me Shintre, come."

Spindle entered the 'Mumbai dome' and was greeted by six other Mumbai boys and a girl,

Rotesh, Kamal, Brajesh, Himesh, Gagan, Karmesh and the girl Sujata. They all shook hands with Spindle, including the girl that offered a rather timid grip, quite appropriate for a girl on meeting a stranger for the first time. They all settled down quite easily and Spindle shared the 'Mumbai' room with Shintre, Rotesh and Kamal. Duties were soon allotted to the boys in the room and Shintre demanded a spotless room, especially the linen that should never be left wet on the bed among other things. Each one was asked to cook on a certain day and the weekends were supposed to be a 'pizza'party with the money being shared among the members of the 'Mumbai' room. Each one was supposed to help clean the room at all times. Alcohol was not a compulsion but strongly recommended. Spindle just lay on the bed that was quite soft and bouncy, unlike what he ha ever witnessed and his sleep was sound at night. Pretty soon the Delhi guys noticed Spindle in a different group and did not like it. They called him the 'rogue' and Spindle just brushed off what he heard from his ear. He was very happy with the Mumbai group and they were kinder and more helpful, especially Shintre and Rotesh. Spindle was asked once to prepare tea for the entire Mumbai group. Spindle knew about a magic technique to prepare tea which he had learnt from his mother. This was the 'fermentation' technique in which you had to leave the tea to brew for fifteen minutes and the final results were bound to be fabulous. And so they were. The entire Mumbai group loved the tea and Sujata stepped out of her room to thank Spindle for the wonderful tea. Spindle became the 'tea' man henceforth and prepared tea for the group, especially in the evenings when the group wanted to rest their tired limbs.

FOUR

THE GAMBLING SPREE

They say that if you have enough money, you can buy America. Money is everything in a place like America. No wonder everyone works very hard to make a million. There are people in such professions as will give them enough money to live and enjoy America which maybe short of a million. There are people that will sell even their bodies to earn a million. Whatever you do, everyone wants to touch the magic figure of a million dollars. Being filthy rich is not a bad thing, but make sure you follow the right path to get there. And if you cannot become filthy rich, then make enough to have fun in a place like America.

The shortest way to make a million is through lottery. There are a million lotteries in America, maybe more, and let's not forget Las Vegas, the gambling capital of the world. Have you been to Las Vegas, well if not then you are missing something. Try your luck at Las Vegas, maybe God will be kind this time. Spindle could never go to Las Vegas and he does not regret it, even one bit. The Mumbai boys once invited Spindle for a trip to Las Vegas that was not far away, and like a dumb ass he refused. In the meantime, the boys always crowded near a small shop that sold lottery tickets. The grand prize was near million dollars and the past did have some winners. Would you believe it, someone actually won a million dollars. What did he do with the money needs no guesses. He probably would have bought a store like the one that sold lottery tickets, or probably a bigger one and multiplied it many times. Or if he were foolish, he would have headed for Las Vegas and lost all the money in gambling. In return the girls probably would have given him the time of his life. The girls all around the world know how to treat millionaires, and probably steal his money and run away.

Before this another incident happened. Spindle once saw his roommate from Delhi walking back too his room rather tired and sweaty. Friendships do not die too soon and Spindle had shared his room for three months before he and Spindle flew to America. Spindle's father also stayed in that room for a while, till the time Spindle recuperated from a nasty accident that Spindle met with just before his trip to America. Well the accident part is a different story which I shall share later somewhere. Spindle stayed in this guy's room and it is said that Spindle got into the bad habit of smoking through this friends of his. But Spindle did not mind and enjoyed his company.

Coming back to America, Spindle as you know had joined the Mumbai guys and so the Delhi guys were pissed off with him. But an old roommate is an old roommate and the friendship never dies, given that you have shared cigarettes with him. Spindle shouted,

"Where have you been Nat?"

"Oh! Hi! Spindle, I just went to the local store. They have given me a job there. I need the money, you see, Spindle, and there's no harm in doing some manual labour."

"But can we work there, given the nature of our entry into this country?"

"Yes, of course, well you decide for yourself. Punjabis run the show there and there's no harm in working hard and earning some money."

"Ok thanks, and you take care. We'll keep meeting, Bye."

It so happened that Spindle stopped himself from walking into that store and asking for a job. He thought it was not right. But given the circumstances and the money he had in his pocket, he decided after a few weeks to walk into the store and see what it was all about. He had even seen the Mumbai boys and a lot of other Delhi boys work there for some pocket money. The manager Mr. Ranbeer Ahluwalia saw Spindle walk into the store rather timidly and great nervousness.

Ranbeer almost yelled,

"Here, how can I help you, son."

"Sir, I heard that you are offering job to students that have recently arrived here and live in the Guesthouse Inns and Suites round the corner. I was thinking if you could also offer me a job?"

"OK, I am very busy right now, please some tomorrow same time, I can see what I can do."

"Right Sir, sorry to bother you."

Next day Spindle arrived at just about the same time he had come the day before. Mr. Ahluwalia was all dressed up and asked Spindle to wait in his office. By the way Ranbeer was all of 26 and Spindle was 29 years old.

"See, the work here is very tough and we need people who can sweat it out. The work is continuous and you will be given a break for just ten minutes when you can do whatever it is that you wish. I want you to walk into the cooler and stack up bottles in the racks for display. The cooler is the toughest part. The temperatures there are as low as -20 degrees centigrade. You can have gloves and let's see how you perform. Tell me right now if you can do it and are willing to do it. Your group is good I must say, but none of them is daring enough to do all the work continuously and on a consistent basis. They come here and do a few things here and there and ask for payment for their labour and then quietly disappear. I do not like that. I want someone to sweat it out with me. I want this store to be the best store in Sant Ana and I pride myself with the work I have done over the years and helped my family and friends. I don't know why I am saying all these things to you, but you seem to be different. As of right now, please jump into the cooler and see if you can handle it. I will first take you around the store and show what all do we sell. Come with me."

Mr. Ahluwalia showed the display section, the slurpy section, coffee section, garbage disposal, the go down where they stored stuff, the cooler where they stacked drinks like beer, red bull, Gatorade, and other aerated and nonaerated drinks, the cash register which Spindle was required to learn in a jiffy, the glass doors at the entrance and in cooler shelves, soda section, the mop that was required to be used every now and again, and some more that made up the small store. The store was not meant for extremely rich people, much like the ones we have in India, but for travellers when they hit the road and are on their way on their SUVs, pick up trucks or fancy cars. Mr. Ahluwalia then showed the huge tobacco section which a hit among the Americans. I guess Americans need them more than anyone else in the world. Fancy cigarette packs of Marlboro reds, Marlboro whites, Virginia Slims, cheap ones too , tobacco sniffs, chewing tobacco and of course nothing is incomplete with cigars.

"Do you smoke?"

"Yes I, do."

"Great."

Mr. Ahluwalia was thrilled to her the reply.

"Why don't you get into the cooler now, real fast and start stacking the new bottles that have just arrived and after that please mop the floor. Thank you."

Spindle walked into the cooler and was snapped a like a cold python around his neck. He felt strangulated and could not breath, it was very cold in there. Yet he kept walking and with great courage started stacking up the bottles one by one. Ranbeer's elder brother Anshu was already in the cooler to help Spindle. Anshu was 29 years old, same age as Spindle.

"Hi, I am Anshu, nice to see you. Are you cold. Just fill up three rows and you are done."

Spindle exceeded expectations, like he always did, when it came to burning within and roughing it out, until he was thrown out of the cooler and handed a mop to clean the floor.

Three more days and Mr. Ranbeer was over the moon. He had found someone that could rough it out and do whatever asked to do with great effort and finesse and never utter a word back in discontent or disgust. The only problem with Spindle, Ranbeer thought was that he always started with a 'NO' when asked to do a job and then eventually did it with great elan, exuberance and excitement.

The Mumbai boys often bought lottery tickets and crowded up the store to watch the results each evening on the big TV screen in the store. They never won anything and wasted their money. They were in and out of the store while Spindle got a full-time job at the store and Ranbeer just loved the boy. Fresh tickets were issued in the morning and the results were declared in the evening. There was always a winner, someone, somewhere, in California, but it was never one of the Delhi or the Mumbai boys. Spindle too once or twice bought the tickets knowing that he will never win the grand prize. Ranbeer often took a break from work and pulled out Spindle for a smoke along with Anshu.

FIVE

SPINDLE AND THE DUMPSTER

Mr. Ahluwalia was quite impressed with Spindle, but he never let Spindle know. Three months at the University had done no good to Spindle. He attended the morning class with the entire group of ten Delhi boys and ten Mumbai boys to study Embedded Systems. But the subject seemed far fetched and hard to grasp. Yet, Spindle listened very carefully in class and tried hard to understand the subject and take down notes. Once in a while he would stand up and raise a question until the boys just smirked and could not bear Spindle standing up and raise a question, when they had none.

After class Spindle ran to the store to meet Mr. Ahluwalia.

"Come on Spindle, you are very late today."

Spindle first was given thick paper to run over the glass doors and windows of the store. He was given a unform that luckily fit him. It was just a small red jacket that had the company logo. Spindle gave it all, his strength, his heart, his honesty, his luck to whatever was thrown at him. That is the reason why he was liked and much appreciated. Once Mr. Ranbeer quietly whispered into his ears,

"Do you know why we like you."

"Please let me know."

"No, we won't, please don't waste time, there's a lot of work to be done."

Spindle mopped the floor, fixed the slurpy machine with huge bags of flavoured liquids in the small room next to the office, where the owner of the store Mr. Randheer Singh sat. Mr. Ahluwalia just happened to be the manager of the store, if I have not mentioned it earlier. Spindle was asked to wash used glasses, flatten the boxes by cutting them with a sharp blade, stacking up the cooler, every now and again, and the most interesting job in the store, handling the cash register. The boys just wanted to do just that and lined up in plenty to do it, where they got to meet customers, many of them sweet and beautiful ladies and young girls. Nobody wanted to do the dirty job that Spindle did, which meant that their time in the store was short lived and very soon they left, all of them, and came in just to do some odd job and earn some money for cigarettes, beer or gambling. Spindle went deep into his job, shuttling to and fro to his college and running in to fix his apron or jacket and diving in before Mr. Ahluwalia could spot him. Spindle was soon on a salary and Mr. Ahluwalia was beginning to like Spindle and the way he went about in his duties with such enthusiasm and excitement. Pretty soon Spindle learnt to prepare coffee and the fifty different flavours of coffee that was prepared in the store with a huge coffee machine.

The coffee was dark and had many flavours. One could add 'cream' or milk into the coffee called 'Half and Half' that came in small cup satchels as per requirement. Spindle liked plain coffee, without any flavour, but with a lot of milk and some sugar. He made he had a cup of coffee in the evening during breaks and smoked a cigarette with Anshu or sometimes even with Mr. Ahluwalia. Soon Spindle learnt almost all there was to learn, very quickly, when he was introduced to the dumpster. It was a huge dumpster and was required to be cleared every morning. Spindle obliged and after the huge crane emptied the dumpster and took all the trash away, Spindle jumped into the dumpster and cleaned it with a mop until it was sparkling clean. Spindle slowly got the name 'The dumpster man' and every morning Spindle cleaned the two dumpsters that the store had. Mr. Ranbeer was elated. He rewarded Spindle with sandwiches, some chocolate donuts and coffee.

SIX
THE STORE

The store in sunny California served a very small purpose, that of providing little things that didn't cost much to people that were not quite well off. It became a hit for travellers that were on the road or were planning to hit the road very soon, for a long trip to paradise, maybe. It was slightly more expensive than the ninety-nine cents store but smaller in size. It was primarily run by Punjabis from India who held franchise all over California. The owner of the chain was most certainly an American and had given these Punjabis to run the store their own way. There were random checks on the store including the dreaded auditor. It was the toughest period for any owner even if he knew he had not misused the store resources or money for his own personal gains. It was like a final exam and if the owner failed then there was a possibility of the store being take away from him and even to the extent of him been put behind bars for fraud.

The owner of the store Mr. Randheer Singh was very worried and upset during the time of audit. Random checks that were not strictly audits were easy to negotiate, but audits meant someone asking the reason for the extra pin that was ordered without being recorded or an invoice prepared for such a purchase. It was nerve wracking and Mr. Randheer just poured out all his frustration and anger on his manager that offered him many cups of coffee and cakes and pastries to appease him,

"Ranbeer, I don't need all this, take it away, please. Give me some peace here. If I fail, we'll both go to jail. And I am warning you Ranbeer, I shall ruin your career, I promise. Then you can beg on the streets, play some music and sing songs with Anshu on the crossroads and the railway stations and earn a nickel or a dime. Please do not let me down. You don't know who you are dealing with, mister."

As luck would have it, the auditor could not find the extra 'pin' in the inventory and the store remained unblemished always before the auditor was shown the door with a chocolate croissant and coffee cup in his hands.

"Ranbeer baby, let me kiss you. You always manage to save me, don't you. I am going to give you an expensive gift, you and Anshu both. We're going to have to have a party tonight at my home, Sharda will be happy too. Please come, I'm leaving."

Ranbeer Ahluwalia was over the moon. He and Anshu jumped in the air and Spindle did not fully understand why the wave of such happiness had hit rather glum faces.

"Spindle, we need to work harder. I want this store to be the best in Orange County. You are good, no doubt, but you need to work even harder, do you get it, son."

The store had a lot of small items like medicines, stationery, garden tools, seeds, machine tools like spanners, screw drivers, wrench, cosmetics for women, dresses like T-shirts, skirts, essentially a potpourri of essentials that did not cost much. You could just come in, have a coffee, a beer, or some high caffeine drink to stiffen your eyes and body, Gatorade, aerated drinks, slurpy, some nachos with cheese which the Mexicans loved very much, sausages of pork, beef and chicken, etc.

Ranbeer asked Spindle to keep all the small medicine boxes, bottles front faced, so that the customer had no problem in looking at the labels and could spot something that they urgently required. After all the world is in a hurry and they have no time to waste their time in a small store, when all this and much more is easily available at a bigger mega store. Besides who could forget the huge collection of sandwiches, donuts, sushi, egg sandwiches, croissants, all carrying an expiry date. The store was supposed to dump the expired sandwiches and other food items into the trash can. No item that had expired should be displayed on the shelf. Ranbeer and the Indian way of doing things tossed a few sandwiches, donuts, etc that had just expired to Spindle and he and Anshul had it too. The store required constant cleaning and so there were men employed to do the same.

SEVEN

SPINDLE AND NIGHT SHIFTS

Three months at the store meant that the time had come for the groups of ten Delhi boys and ten Mumbai boys to leave for home. Spindle too was to leave. His father once called him up from India while Spindle was busy with store work and Spindle told him he was at the college. Spindle did not want his father to know that he had joined the store and had started earning a few bucks. Father would be hurt to hear about Spindle's occupation and may even prevent him from working at the store. Father missed Spindle a lot and wanted his boy back again at home.

Spindle walked lazily that afternoon to the store for his last shift but was happy to head home to his father. He knew that his father missed him too much and could not survive without him.

"Why are you so sad, Spindle? What happened?"

"Mr. Ranbeer, I am leaving. I must catch the night flight with the boys and head home. I have completed my three months at the University and got the certificate that I had come here for. Maybe I'll land up a job somewhere in Embedded Systems. Besides I must go to my father right away. I cannot see him all alone."

"Spindle, don't be sad. I have a plan for you. Why don't you take admission in UC Riverside, which is not very far from here in their Extension for another certificate program. You can easily get your student visa extended. Don't worry about the cost. I have already talked to the owner and he had agreed to lend the money for your certificate program. How does it sound? Son, we need you here. I will take good care of you, I promise. Very soon we are going to have a major inspection by the head of the chain store. If we get selected then our store will become the best store in Orange County and will get a huge grant which will be beneficial to all of us, including you. Don't say no, please. I want you around here. You are my best employee."

Spindle too had come to America for the first time and didn't want to leave too soon. Somewhere deep inside he wanted to stay back and experience America closely. After some thought Spindle agreed to stay back,

"OK, Sir, if you insist. I will stay back for three more months. But I must get my papers straight."

"Great, I'll help you with the papers. And you can pay back the owner by working at the store. Isn't that a great deal."

It was a sad parting and the boys came to Spindle in turns. It was two o' clock in the morning and the boys tried to explain to Spindle that he has no future here. A big cultural shock was enough to leave this place and head homewards. There is no concept of family here and children just do not connect with their parents. They run away from homes and do what they please. Girls here dress like they have shortage of clothes and affairs are like an everyday thing. The food is hard to digest and sweet is sweeter than sweet, its very harmful to say the least. People here use very foul language and they have no culture. There's never anyone on the streets, unlike the bazaar we have in India. This is a very lonely place and the only company you have is probably your pet or your car. Here cars are like water, everywhere you look, you'll only find cars especially at a place like California. People have beer and Coca Cola instead of water, its cheaper than water. Here Indians are not treated with respect and there's no point in staying in an alien land where you are not respected and not wanted around to say the least. Return to India. There you will find everything you are looking for, including a good job and lots of money.

Spindle listened and spot argued until about four in the morning. But he had already made up his mind and it was not wrong when his father called him an 'obstinate' guy. The morning came and the guys were on their beds, trying to get some sleep. That evening they were to catch the evening flight to India with the usual stop over somewhere.

Spindle walked gingerly to the store and helped himself with a warm cup of coffee after getting there. Mr. Ahluwalia called him,

"Spindle, the owner would like to speak to you. Please come to the office."

"Spindle, we have seen your work in the last three months. We have decided to offer you a loan for studies at UC Riverside for a quarter. You can pay us back by working here. We are not asking you to sign any papers, just that you must pay your debts. For that we want you to do graveyard shifts for about two months. That will easily cover your debts. I know it's hard. You will be the only one present at the store at night and you have to manage the store without any sleep. That is what is a graveyard shift. Are you ready. We have a shortage of staff with us and Ranbeer is too tied up with store work and so is Anshu. We'll help you with your admission." Mr. Randheer, the owner was clear with his proposal.

"Yes sir, I will do what is required."

"That is what I expected from you. Good."

The boys left that night with Spindle by their side.

"You are making a big mistake, Spindle."

Spindle went back to his night shifts.

EIGHT

DEEP CUT BELOW THE PINKY FINGER

Spindle had learnt the odd jobs of mopping the floor and filling up coffee, arranging the display of varied bottles, filling up cans and plastics bottles of drinks, alcoholic and non-alcoholic, cleaning glass with dry paper after spraying solution on the glass, pushing random buttons on the cash register to help customers buy products, flattening boxes of cardboard to be discarded, cleaning shelves of food items and a lot other things that required constant vigil.

Night shifts were sometimes scary, with the cops around, and then a deadly silence with no one to be found until dawn. Sometimes someone would turn up with nothing to buy in particular, just an unusual night walk to the store to ease a rather sick mind. A lady once came along with her pickup and parked herself at the door. She was high on some kind of drug and very unhappy with herself and her life. She stood there watching her pickup for hours while Spindle was busy negotiating store work, including making entries on a register of the entire sale that day. It's a sad tale for many people like this all over the world. It's not all glamour and glitzy, like we were living in heaven in perfection, right from our bodies, mind and soul. Many are living in total darkness when their minds have stopped functioning normally, or they have some kind of grave addiction that they cannot get over. Is it very surprising that people in America, and perhaps all over the world, greet each morning like a brand-new day in paradise when they have everything they can dream of. People think that way about America and want to come here and live forever like a king or a queen. But when someone comes and lives here, they only see darkness all around, be it California or New York. What we see is not true and Spindle had begun to see the real side of America after working at the store for over three months. He had seen such darkness that was not there in his own country and sometimes thought that he had made a big mistake by not catching the plane with the boys back home and listened to Mr. Ahluwalia, getting unnecessarily stuck in a debt situation.

It was past midnight. There was no one at the store. Spindle had begun his nightly activities that will not allow him rest even for a minute. Besides he could not just leave the store and step out when there was no one there. He began by filling up condiments like mustard sauce for the nachos, jalapenos, chopped onion and tomato that came in small plastic bags, pickled cucumber and so on. He did not like all of them personally and could not understand how people liked some odd vegetable that was boiled and pickled. He then quickly ran the mop over the floor when not even the cops were in sight. Coffee was to be prepared early morning and the cold drinks too were to be stacked when they got a fresh supply. Donuts and pastries were delivered early morning by the donut truck. The days account register had to be updated that that too could wait for at least one hour. Spindle thus decided to flatten the cardboard boxes and transfer them to the store before they would find their way into the dumpster or maybe put to some use that the manager thought fit.

Spindle had always been a day dreamer all his life. That is the reason why he often failed to concentrate on the work at hand or maybe appear at an examination totally lost in his own world. There was no dearth of intelligence but somehow Spindle always ranked in the lower half of any class.

Spindle had a very sharp blade in his hand while he ran it through stiff cardboard to flatten the boxes at hand. Suddenly the blade slit the skin under the pinky finger in a long cut. The white portion under the skin had become visible and Spindle was bleeding profusely. He ran to the store for some cloth to stop the bleeding, which would not cease. He opened the first aid box for some cotton and sat with his would for over an hour, washing it with water every now an again. Finally the bleeding stopped, but Spindle could still see the white portion under the skin.

Spindle somehow completed the rest of the work with ginger hands and waited for someone to appear. At the stroke of seven in the morning Mr. Ahluwalia stepped in and was shocked to see the wound on Spindle's hand,

"Spindle, my God! What happened to you. Silly boy, why didn't you call me at night. You know this could turn septic. How can you be so irresponsible. We have to rush you to the hospital."

Spindle was rushed to the nearby hospital and given stitches on the left palm. The owner took him to the hospital and paid all expenses.

"Please, Spindle please take care of yourself. Do not work so hard that you hurt yourself. I don want such a thing to happen again, you hear?"

With time Spindle's wound healed. He continued with night shifts.

NINE

SABOBA CASINO

It is hard to gauge a person and his or her true self. Many people follow the route of not trusting anyone they meet. For if they trust someone too much and that person happens to be a crook then they are hard done for. Hence right from childhood they get into the habit of not trusting anyone. Sometimes their parents teach them the same thing. Majority of the people in the world fall into the above category and it is surely the right way forward, for people can be misleading, no matter how they look and behave.

Spindle was more of the foolish kind. He had developed the habit of trusting people blindfolded. That does not mean that he trusted anyone and everyone that he met. He trusted those that were good to him and helped him in some way in his life, not caring too much about what they did when they were not with him. Hence, he trusted Mr. Ahluwalia who over the months had helped him immensely, firstly by giving him a job at his store and making him earn some money and later on getting him admission at UC Riverside. Mr. Ahluwalia as mentioned was a few years younger than Spindle and Mr. Ahluwalia's elder brother Anshu was Spindle's age. Spindle had learnt 'trust' from his mother. He trusted and that is the reason why he was used, met with an accident, became addicted to smoking and took pills to stay calm. The problem with trusting and listening to the heart is that it often gives us misery and strife and sometimes there is great danger of falling apart at the hands of the 'turned out to be' crook. Mr. Ahluwalia would often talk about his sexual exploits, listen to Hip Hop artists like Eminem, Snoop Dogg and talk about someone by the name of Tupac Shakur. Spindle listened to them and liked the music, although the words were rather vulgar, he thought. He even drank some vodka mixed with orange juice as Mr. Ahluwalia drove his metallic yellow Honda Civic across town, sometimes all the way to downtown LA.

It had been long enough for some kind of friendship to develop between Spindle and Mr. Ahluwalia. Those long rides at night when store work and college were forgotten or aptly dealt with and put to rest, these buddies swept the night on the car with the metallic sheen with cigarettes and a drop of alcohol. The light just soothed the eye and all one could hear was the shrill of cars passing by, new and old, by the window on the hard highway.

On a weekend when Spindle was let go of his duties for the night, Mr. Ahluwalia drove his car all the way to Saboba Casino, about forty odd miles from the store. Spindle had no clue where the duo was headed and Mr. Ahluwalia never disclosed a secret. He just went high on hip hop, Cigarettes and all and Spindle carried no qualms of his undying curiosity, he just joined in. The singer being too loud shook the window panes, like the throbbing woofer of a speaker, but was too far from it being smashed to pieces. The car and the highway, so symbolic of America, when people forget their very being, especially on weekends, and become the grave sinner that they always desired to be. Mr. Ahluwalia drove the car not less than seventy miles an hour, cruise control, with magical fingers and a ranting Eminem, pissed off over something, the way he always is.

They reached the infamous Saboba casino that don the colours of pleasure and more on a Saturday night, with the neon lights and ladies dressed in scanty tops and stockings, high heels and carrying trays of orange punch and some pistachios. Mr. Ahluwalia headed straight for a game of black jack while Spindle just stood agape not knowing what to do until he was pushed forward by the hand by Mr. Ahluwalia. Spindle was thrown into the room with plenty of slot machines. He knew nothing of slot machines, and so he decided to ask his fellow brother, some stranger, that was working hard at a slot machine,

"I was wondering, Sir , if you could teach me..."

"Get off me, dumb ass. Don't you see, I am busy here."

Spindle was upset. He sat at an vacant slot machine and decided to try his luck. Twenty, another twenty, a ten, a five, one dollar, the slot machine gulped everything that Spindle had and gave back nothing. Spindle then checked his pocket, all he had was a quarter, that he did not want to lose. He joined Mr. Ahluwalia at the black jack table. Mr. Ahluwalia was quite an expert, as he tapped at the table like a pro and had won some money too. The game carried on until about three in the morning with the ladies too happy to serve for all the money that was, they got by selling juices and nuts. Mr. Ahluwalia finally gave up. He had lost everything he earned over a month. There was no point in carrying on. The casino looked bare and Mr. Ahluwalia wanted to reach the store before dawn. He sped past the highway, while Spindle enjoyed the fresh morning air. They were back home in no time. Mr. Ahluwalia promised Spindle to take him to the casino again sometime.

TEN
THE SIX FLAGS TRIP

Saboba was a delight. Mr. Ahluwalia promised Spindle a second trip soon. In the meantime, Spindle was asked to learn the game of black jack. Casino in the latter half of the night is not a pretty sight. There are men dozing off on the floor, too drunk to help themselves out of the main door of the casino. They sure lose all the money they had and start again a pauper. No one has ever walked out of the casino with a windfall or gains from gambling. A winner in pursuit is always tempted to try again and win an amount that he has unheard of. That amount could make him a king and he never has to work anymore. But that somehow never happens. He plays and plays until the alcohol pushes him through astounding gains to great losses, until he has gives away the money that he initially had when he came to the casino. Mr. Ahluwalia always lost everything that he had, but still was buoyed by the Friday night with pretty girls and flashy cars and that hope that people in dire need of money always had.

There are many attractions in America, especially at a place like California. The Disney land, water parks, huge aquariums, mountains and of course Six Flags magic mountain. The twenty boys from Mumbai and Delhi once decided to make a trip to the Six Flags magic mountain. It is an entertainment park and Spindle too joined the boys for the trip. He had no idea what an entertainment park meant. It was a day trip and the boys got up pretty early for a free morning breakfast. It was a sunny day and the sky was pure blue. In California they say that the sun shines for three hundred days in a year. That is pretty high, given that in India the sun shines on a clear blue sky for a few days at a stretch until grey clouds cover the horizon without any precipitation. Here getting clear blue sky with the sun was magical, what with the air so clean and healthy. This is perhaps one of the big reasons why people from far away countries, especially India, like to come here and settle for good. Besides there are not many people that live here in a gigantic country. The Americans are wise not to allow a lot of people into their country.

The boys planned a trip to the Six Flags Magic Mountain in a hurry, mid-session. They were to leave early Friday and return on a Sunday. Spindle had never heard of such a thing in his life and his own town sometimes had the 'mela' where you could try the desi 'Ferris wheel', play the game of throwing a ring round the neck of some dummy, shoot bullets at assorted balloons, shake hands with the jester with a silly face, try street food at its very best or of you are old enough, you could check out the ladies who just 'happened' to pass by. This was a deserted place like all of America is. Spindle had some inkling of parks, of entertainment parks, and magic parks and water parks but had never been to one. He had decided to stay put and enjoy the delicacies that it had to offer on very neat stalls with fancy women in stockings and red lips greeted all with a smile. He wished he could steal one of those and run away to his home land for good.

The weather was nice like always on a Friday morning. The classes had been negotiated in a hurry and the boys boarded the bus that had its engine at the back for a round trip to Six Flags. The crystal blue skies and the sun a warm yellow dazzled in Spindle's eyes when he longed for a touch of their warmth. If anyone were to get a taste of the real 'heaven', California was the place, albeit with one difference, the people. The huge bus wagged its tail left and right and brought the rest of the traffic to a standstill on those turns, covering a huge area. It's sound was more like a dinky car and brought memories to those that have played with them in their childhood. It's speed was never too much and it gripped the road as it moved along, with wide rolling alloy wheels. The boys broke into song and dance and pulled the lone girl with her sweet voice. The clapping and the beat made the journey bearable with lots of bags of chips, nachos and the like ripped open and consumed. Spindle was rather shy, didn't want to sing or clap. He just looked out of the window to see the quiet bus tread on a familiar path and the surrounding breeze speaking of glorious days to remember and hold in his memory forever. California had been memorable so far and there were many moments in time that Spindle remembered and it did not come as a surprise when a few of his friends vowed to never leave this land.

Six Flags magic mountain arrived and the boys were knocked off their feet. There was a huge gate and it was like a grand entrance into a palace. What with gold, silver and precious shining metal embroidered, very soon the boys were pushing themselves in. As usual the gang stopped at an ice cream parlour, within the premises. Along with the cream lick of delight there were some nice girls at the counter. They always had a smile and some of the boys just could not help exchanging words with them. Somone pointed out from the back the girls could not get a word the boys said. It was Indian English and sometimes hard to understand by the white people. The boys just turned around and made plans for the day. There were rides to take that came to their mind. Everyone barring one and Spindle wanted to stay away from the rides,

"Why you chicken, are you scared."

"Well, not at all."

"Then why don't you come with us, Spindi."

"Sure, if you want me to."

Spindle joined the boys, not because he wanted to or because he loved to, but because the boys threw a challenge he could not refuse.

One ride after the other. Each was even more dangerous than the previous one. It is funny to see that little kids of the age group of five or six had not hesitation to take the rides. They were strapped nicely and their bodies filled less than half their seats. When the ride began, they did not shout or scream, like they had been hypnotized before the ride. The rest of the people screamed as if they were going to die.

The first ride was a speed check ride. You were to sit on a horizontal wagon. It started without speed, like a train that has begun to roll after sitting for hours at a railway platform. It picked up speed slowly and at one moment it could gather great speed, enough to make all scream like in hell. In just a few seconds it did just that and Spindle poured out all the invectives that he knew. He was scared of the strap around his shoulders and waist getting unhooked and he did cry for dear life. It went around three circles and the speed kept going up. The boys were sweating cold with fear and the screams went loud enough for miles to hear. After three circles of hell the thing suddenly stopped, like it had never started. All boys just got back their breath, ran their hands over faces of sweat and smiled like they had great fun. And fun it was. Spindle discovered a new side of himself, the adventurous side. He didn't know he had capacity to go such manic levels, having done crazier things in his life.

Then came the next one and then the next one. In one the aspirants were seated on a chair and strapped enough. The chair was then lifted vertically to the height of a tall sky scraper. It just went going up and up and Spindle was just getting too nervous. The boys just laughed at the desperation of Spindle, like they knew the feeling. But inside each one was scared as hell, just that Spindle had never learnt the art of hiding his true feelings behind a mask. Finally, the chair locked high in the air and the laughs just doubled. Spindle wanted to touch the ground with his feet and was not amused at this kind of perversion. Fun is fine but they were stretching it too far, he thought. The chairs were released and they came down with great force, as if they would hit the ground with great force. Every one tore their own jacket of screams, crying loud for dear life. The chairs came down together, bounced up and was thrown to a lesser height than before. A few more bounces and it lay static on the floor. All were unstrapped and had a great laugh at Spindle's expense. Spindle held his breath and was happy that the machine did not break down while the pullies suffered great pressure. The next ride was the most dangerous ride that Spindle had ever seen. He just walked with the boys to the ride, even though he had been reluctant initially to try these deadly rides. This one had a trolley in which sat all the passengers, strapped nicely. It moved slow initially and pretty soon slanted sideways. Suddenly, like someone pulled the lever, it picked up great speed and ran higher and higher along a curvy path. The path changed its course every second. Very soon the visitors were as high as hundred feet above the ground. Spindle gripped the chair as hard as he could and it felt as if he could touch the skies. He stayed still and waited. Within a few seconds the trolley came down and locked itself at the station. The boys got out and lost their speech for moments. It was the most exciting thing anyone of the twenty boys had ever seen. Back home there was nothing like this, the boys were convinced. The next ride was even more dicey although it had nothing to do with heights. Spindle was not willing to try any ride but a soft nudge on his shoulders was enough for him to give in. The takers of the ride were seated aptly and strapped with assurance like always. Spindle did not expect much from this ride and that he could manage this one with ease. Little did he know, for when the button was pushed, the trolley with the passengers swept around crazily with great speed. Sometimes they were upside down, sometimes sideways, but never in a straight line. It ran as if it would never stop. No one had time to scream and shout, it just kept coming and coming. Ten minutes of disaster, that's what Spindle called it, and never forgot this particular ride, for it was the most dangerous among all. Such craziness can only be found in America. They can do anything, anywhere in a culture of 'act whacky if you can', that they call 'freedom'.

ELEVEN

THE SECOND QUARTER

Spindle embarked on his first journey to UC Riverside. The manager dropped Spindle at a railway station. Spindle walked out of the car and looked puzzled. The building he was pointed to looked like some kind of a fancy hotel. He turned around to the manager to make sure if it was the right building. Mr. Ahluwalia bade goodbye and turned his car around for the store. Spindle gingerly walked to the entrance to find huge white walls of architecture. The floor was shining like it had been unboxed right then. There were counters with magical yellow lights illuminating things shining like gold. There were food items, nicely packed, coffee cups so white, next to shining coffee machines. The air was fragrant and clean as a whistle. Everything around looked so bright and cheerful. Very few people took the train, it seemed. The tickets were big and rectangular with print on scented paper. Had Spindle suddenly ambled on heaven. The light posts were tall and black, clean and tipped by a bright shining white light that was blazing in radiant glow. He got his tickets at the counter and the train was due in twenty minutes. He had time enough for a walk to the shops for goodies and a cup of hot coffee. He had never seen such a railways station in his life. The cakes at the counter were fresh out of the oven, it seemed, and the taste was mush and cream like his teeth would sink in them. The coffee was bitter but hot and fresh. He sat on a long chair that had a beautiful shape, with arms wanting to hug someone and show its love. Its hollow was slanting downwards as if to hold its guest tightly. Spindle just sat on the edge, looking around with a constant eye on his watch. There was complete silence around. Everyone quietly went about their business. Back home a railway station meant complete mayhem. Everyone ran for no reason. Even then a lot of people missed their trains. The reason was the huge crowd that gathered every moment at the station. Many were local, many long distance and for many it was their only home. Out here people were more civilized and there was no rush. The train would come and very few passengers would get in to occupy a near empty train. Spindle walked the turn next to the tracks in the last five minutes. He helped himself with some orange soda as the weather got hotter. There were a few more that were to take the train, standing beside him. The train approached with a loud sound and a heavy load. It stopped for less than a minute and took Spindle away to Riverside. The air blew softly like a favourite melody. People looked gay, holding hot cups and softly chatting. They were the office goers that found the train a better choice than cars. The gentlemen had ties that gently flew off its place as the train moved on its tracks. They constantly put their ties down and discussed light matters without bothering about what happened around them. Spindle looked out of the train that passed through pastures, tall buildings, gardens, a spell of trees with leaves that jumped as the train hit them with a gust. It was going to take about one hour to get at the gates of the college and Spindle enjoyed the moments that swept past him. He knew that he would never forget these moments in his lifetime and the grand railway station, unlike what he had known about railway stations and seen it before his eyes. There was plenty to eat here and live by. America thus is a magnet that attracts young people. If bitten by the American bug, it is very difficult to go anywhere else. This place takes in people from all over and offers a grand and safe home. The train slowed down somewhere along the path making a few people get up from their seats and adjust their clothes. Some took a walk to the exit door and looked at the fine weather that had a touch of warmth. The usual clicking sound was heard as the train progressed further in its path. The huge horn blew loud for all to hear.

By the time the train halted, Spindle had lived through one of the best experiences of his life. The train journey would never end. It wanted to show more than can be seen. A train ride such as this can be something to remember. A train ride much like this, when the wheels must roll and we sit in patience and enjoy our stay. A life of patience and perseverance shall get us where we ought to be. We just need to be on board and wait till the very end. Sometime, somewhere we shall reach the end. The train with its one-track motion must be observed and lived through in silence. The final bend shall come after miles of journey. We must busy ourselves and let eternity flow. There was a bus station just outside the train station. Spindle got on to the bus that were just like anywhere else in California.

The highlight of his three-month course at Riverside Extension was his French class and the fact that Mr. Ahluwalia rode miles at night to pick up Spindle and ride home. There were no trains available at night to take him home. Neither was there any bus service. Mr. Ahluwalia, however, could not leave his employee stranded by night.

"I never do this much for anyone. I don't know why I cannot help driving all the way just to pick you up. You are a good lad."

The French class was like a whiff of cool breeze. Spindle signed up for it. It was not a compulsory course. There was a French teacher by the name of Danielle with big blue eyes. The classroom had a bunch of kids, eager to speak the most romantic language of all. Danielle gave French names to all her students. Spindle was Jean, pronounced with a hollow throat. Danielle warned all that French was not an easy language to master. The right French required some vocal training and the vocal cords passed through some unusual stretching. The real French was not from the mouth but from the inner. It meant that French was a language of the heart. The lips and the tongue had a secondary role to play. All beautiful languages of the world require great effort and practice and hence is perfected by few. The warnings of Danielle were like a sword that pierced through the hope that Spindle had of ever learning the language. Yet he sat there looking at her eyes and the whiteness of Daniell's skin. The beauty with which she uttered every word. Her smile was reassuring that the students would take home something precious when they leave. Spindle just did not care if he failed. He loved her and tried to utter words that he had never heard. Danielle appreciated the effort even though she knew it was never going to make Spindle speak correctly. The students were shown short clips of people talking in French on the TV. The other students too found it difficult to speak words that were new to them. The inner job was a lot tougher than uttering words that required little or no effort. Americans do not follow the conventional way of speaking English. They have shortened it to their comfort and utter several words in one breath. It is hard for an outsider to catch what is thrown at them. But with time they too learn the lean and mean way to speak English. French needs too much effort but it produces great sounds. English language has adopted many French words and they seem to be popular. Especially in parties when guests need to be impressed for personal gains.

There was a total of six students including Spindle in the French class. The class continued for three months. Spindle made no progress. He just liked to watch Danielle and smell the fragrance of her perfume. Her smiles to blank faces and a constant discouragement were well received. Tipped with hope that things would be easier as time went along. Like in many classes of several things before in his life, Spindle just sat through it. The main course too was in full swing and come evening, the place was lit by beautiful white and yellow lights. There were cafes lined up on the other side of the main road calling for some romance. There were restaurants that served Indian food too. The marketplace was packed of goodies and little things that make life a little more bearable. And they do not cost much. Spindle would often sit at the café after his French class, waiting for the car of Mr. Ahluwalia to pick him up. There were young girls and boys huddled over cream and coffee, talking softly and smiling every second. Spindle wondered is someone was there for him too. Evening is the best time for everyone it seems. It is the time to forget about the load over one's shoulder and enjoy the light and fragrant air. The twilight is perhaps the most romantic and couples just have to take a walk together and renew their promises.

The French class was now coming to an end and so was the main subject in the certificate program. Spindle had gotten used to the train ride and he just knew where to go and when in order to get to his destination. He had become familiar with the trees and grass, the evenings under beautiful lights, the girls skimpily dressed, interlocking fingers with their mates. Last of all the blessed car of Mr. Ahluwalia to pick him up for the graveyard shift at the store.

As a final assignment, Danielle asked all his students to prepare a passage in French. All of the students would be given a chance to read out their written passage in the final class. Spindle had not understood a word of French. He didn't know what to do. He decided to write something in English and use the translator to translate it in French.

On the final day Danialle walked into the class a little sad. She knew she would never see her students again. The students greeted her and got to their jobs right away. Everyone had prepared something and Danialle was so proud. When all that had prepared their passage were through, Danielle bade goodbye to each one of them.

"I hope to see you again, soon. Goodbye."

Spindle walked out of the class disappointed. He never got up to read his passage that he had prepared. Many months later Spindle received an email from the French teacher that was addressed to all the students. She thanked them again and would like to see them learn the language soon. Spindle replied to her email, saying that he had prepared a passage in French that he wanted to read out that evening. But did not.

"Silly Jean. You should have told me, child. What have you done. You can still send the passage by email. I would love to read it."

Thus ended Spindle's French class and his second quarter. A third one was on its way soon.

TWELVE
THE THIRD SEASON

Mr. Ahluwalia wanted Spindle to stay.

"Have you heard of the possible work permit that after three quarters at the university."

"That is exciting, Sir. I can arrange the fees for the third quarter but the papers need to be fixed."

"O! I will help you with that, Spindle. Stay with me a little longer. Students come to me and leave some day. I want you to stay for as long as you can."

The papers were not a problem. UC Extension had a separate building from the main university. It was a beautiful compound with trees, cemented passage, shops, a ballet hall, garden chairs to sit outside or under the tree if desired. Spindle had evening classes. He started in the afternoon, riding on the bus, all the way to the gates of the university. The class was scheduled for five in the evening, although sometimes the students arrived late and the class was either postponed or started late by sixish. By the time the class was over, darkness set in and the lights were aglow all around the compound. It was a most beautiful picture to behold, what with the wind and the swaying leaves on wholesome trees. It was a dream ride home on the bus with white lights and yellow lights all along the way. They dazzled in the eye of the gazer and soothed the senses. Life was then just a glimpse of the bright, cheerful and the rest just an unnecessary baggage.

Arriving at three meant walking about for sometimes he even took the noon bus to the extension.

Spindle walked up to the ice cream parlour. The heat made those large scoops of yogurt ice cream tempting. He sat under the tree to enjoy the dripping delight. There was a rush at that store in that period. Grownups, little ones, crowded the small shop with their hands stretched to the hilt. Spindle was all of twenty-nine. He never looked into the eyes of beauty for an opening. No girl ever did the same. They just walked past him, looking rather aloof. Spindle had never fallen in love, or so he believed. Every hour, every minute was a breeze of hope that swung his cone of yogurt ice cream. He just licked his stuff and his eyes just went around like that of a watch tower. It fell on pretty faces and God's creations, too uppity and high class. A stranger from a faraway land was an illusion. A place with a dearth of hearts. That's America. A little hall with young girls with their ballet tutored by grown up women. The girls and the women wore the usual costume and swung their arms and legs to the music. They swung their hips and sat on the floor with legs stretched in a straight line. They had little frocks hanging around their waists and it floated high with every hip swing. Their soles had the end of their costume in a lace. Spindle watched them very carefully. The music in the ballet hall was almost inaudible. All he saw was the girls and their heavenly flight. He could afford to spend the whole afternoon watching the girls and their group. Sometimes he would take off earlier than required in the noon bus. The shutters were down but yogurt ice cream shop was open. The girls appeared to be like dolls of glass, beautiful yet made of stone.

Mr. Wu made his way each evening for a class of Oracle DBA. He lived near the university. He was Vietnamese. He had worked his way up the ladder of becoming one of the geniuses of IT, especially in DBA. He was called for lectures far and wide. He would often say,

"A little tweak and in goes a million dollars in my pocket."

He was an expert in his subject and big companies had found a proven way to fix bugs and blockages in running code. There were boys and girls that attended his class. They wanted to learn the inner working of a Data Base. Spindle too tried all his might at learning the basics of DBA. Then the evening would arrive and the cool winds took over. The bus ride home was like sailing on a calm sea. The trees were dark green in the bright lights and the road a streak of black. Spindle did not get far with DBA. He had work waiting for him at the store. The work increased with time as he became skilled. Nobody knew that one fine day Spindle would leave. Mr. Ahluwalia certainly didn't. He was assuming that Spindle would find a way to be with him forever. And then Mr. Ahluwalia would promote Spindle and increase his pay. Mr. Ahluwalia did not want to hand over the tally gun yet to Spindle. The tally gun was digital and it kept a record of all the products present in the store and worked out what was needed. It was completely based on the sales pattern of each product in the store. Mr. Ahluwalia was too eager to teach every nitty gritty of the store to Spindle. What with the preparation of an auspicious day for the store when the head of the chain of the store was invited to this store. Mr. Ahluwalia needed Spindle and all his staff to prepare the store for the arrival of the head. The store had been performing very well based on the sales generated in the last year. The store was about to be declared the best in the entire county. It was also to receive some grant for the expansion and development of the store and a salary hike for each employee. The store owner was mighty thrilled of the head visit. He gave strict instructions to Mr. Ahluwalia and all its employee to stress on cleanliness of the store. Every nook and cranny were required to be cleaned, washed and sanitized. Some new products were going to be introduced and racks and shelves given a new look. Some new sandwiches were to come in and further addition to coffee flavours were in the offing. The floor of the store was mopped, cleaned and waxed each day to bring a new dazzle and to enhance the shine. Spindle worked on the double and his third quarter at the university was sporadically interrupted. Spindle did not mind, not even the warnings of Mr. Ahluwalia when he sometimes came late to the store in the morning. The customers were secondary now. Many were not allowed to enter. Especially those that just killed time and walked in with dirty shoes. The build up was too harrowing for everyone. All were weary right at the start of the day. Mr. Ahluwalia drank coffee like water and smoked all day long. He dreamt of having his own store one day. Spindle too joined Mr. Ahluwalia until his lung choked with that putrid smoke out of cigarettes.

The big day came. The sky was mirky with smoke like fog. The sun had hidden beneath a thick cloud. It was not very cold and hence thicks jackets were like a misnomer for the cold. It was hot as summer. Maybe because of the head's arrival at a small store. All employees waited and waited buzzing around the entrance. They polished the floor more than maximum possible shine. Spindle stayed back. He walked around the alleys to make sure the shelves on the shop floor were fully stacked. He cleaned with his usual rug and attended to calls from Mr. Ahluwalia.

Soon a man in a black suit, tie, bald, followed by a well-dressed lady walked in. They had a chauffeur driven car and shook hands with the owner, followed by Mr. Ahluwalia. They were the head of the chain. They looked around and walked a few steps into the store. The lady broke into a conversation with the store owner. There were festoons floating in the air, big balloons, like in a birthday party. The head was offered warm coffee and so was his wife. They stayed for about ten minutes and were gone before their coffee turned cold. The whole store had been renovated, revamped for those auspicious steps. It was all over before it even began.

The store got the grant it was looking for. The salaries of each employee were hiked. The owner of the store was happy with his manager. Spindle had tears in his eyes. He looked at Mr. Ahluwalia and prepared for an exit. There were other things that beckoned and he had to leave the store for good. Mr. Ahluwalia knew all about it. He just looked into Spindle's eyes and said,

"If you need a job, son, you know where to go. Take care. And you will never forget me."

THIRTEEN
RIDE TO LA

They wait for Friday. Collect their weekly pay and jump into the freeway. Then this long ride in their worn-out car to LA. Americans call it freedom. Cars run neck to neck in hugging lanes. Spindle once asked Mr. Ahluwalia where these cars were headed,

"Even they don't know, son. We are off to LA. I want to show you what it looks like."

It is like sitting still on the freeway. Like the cars were not moving. And it went on forever.

"They'll probably hit the casino." Mr Ahluwalia cleared the air.

The night spoke of a darkness of velvet, a pleasant breeze, dark green trees. But who was bothered. All they knew that their pockets were far from full. They wanted more 'dope', in the common language for greater fun in life. There were no obstacles on the way to speak of. Mr. Ahluwalia lit the occasional cigarette and passed it on to Spindle. This was the first time Spindle was on a car ride to LA. He had once toured the city on bus. American to him was like a huge concert hall or a stadium with no one in it.

Many hours later Mr. Ahluwalia ran into the city. There were those huge and menacing traffic lights, impressive. They made it very clear to the meagre traffic what to do at the crossroads. Shops lined on both sides of the street that were empty as expected. Big labels that were tossed like candies to the third world meant nothing to the high brow LA public. The owners of such gigantic labels probably had a house or two in LA. Mr. Ahluwalia did not stop his car to enter these heavily scented and chilled shops. They had lights in them that were as powerful as sunlight, probably. Mr. Ahluwalia rode straight to the downtown area. These areas were inhabited by the blacks. They lived in poverty in spite of the affluence around them. They did not do any work and roamed around their neighbourhood skimpily dressed all day. They did drugs and everything in that category. They were the frustrated lot and no one ever crossed their area. The downtown area was theirs and Mr. Ahluwalia took the risk of driving through that area. He stopped his car and lit a cigarette.

"They have been wronged, son, severely wronged. That is all I can tell you."

A black man came running at great speed towards the car. It seemed like he would smash the windscreen with the sharp weapon he carried. Mr. Ahluwalia changed gears and palmed the wheel for a U-turn. He was gone before that man could get to the car.

"Good thing. Mr. Ahluwalia, you had the ignition on."

They swept past the downtown and into the city. A beautiful city of lights and the roads like a ballet floor. But no one to be seen.

"You have to be Buddha to enjoy this city, I can tell you." Mr. Ahluwalia had crossed over to the freeway, lighting a new cigarette every ten minutes. The freeway was long and the car was on cruise control. Mr. Ahluwalia pulled his left leg to the seat cushion and caressed the wheel.

A few months later Mr. Ahluwalia took another trip to LA. This time in broad daylight. He did not disclose the purpose of his visit to Spindle. He just gave Spindle the day off and the two took off to LA. They entered the freeway before Spindle could frame a question for Mr. Ahluwalia. Soon the clucking sounds of the wheels meant that it was going to be a long ride. Their car kept running with cigarettes on each one's lips. There were other cars around with a difference. The people in them showed greater purpose. They preferred to man the car instead of cruise control. Spindle would often turn around to Mr. Ahluwalia with a question mark. Mr. Ahluwalia just let it be and took a long drag on the butt, tossing it out.

LA at noon is beautiful. The sun it almost always out and the air is soft. People are out with huge shopping carts to that trendy market for groceries and stuff. They make sure to bump into wine shacks for some rare wine. The culture of drinking wine was new to Spindle. Probably people loved the after effects of drinking wine. Besides getting tipsy, it brought a sort of heaviness to the inner of their mouths. The after flavour that stayed was most enchanting. There are offices galore in LA. It is the head office of many big companies, firms and big labels. Somehow the air is so pure and inviting that people don't want to leave LA, or the United States in general.

Mr. Ahluwalia was a fast mover and pretty soon parked his car in front of a huge building in a not so busy LA street,

"Wait here kid, I'll be right back."

Spindle didn't want to step out of the car. He just looked at the mechanical shift, accelerator, steering wheel of the car. He had never driven a car before. He constantly asked Mr. Ahluwalia to offer him the wheel and the driver's seat but Mr. Ahluwalia kept putting it off.

Suddenly Mr. Ahluwalia appeared from nowhere and shouted out,

"Brother, I finally got the green card. O! my God this is the greatest day of my life. Let's celebrate. Please light one for me."

The sound box exploded with Eminem and the windows were pulled up. Mr. Ahluwalia went crazy,

"Give me some Chingy tonight, my Pal!"

Both went happy back home and that night was spent in the local Casino with drinks and the rest.

FOURTEEN

MRS. TURNER AT THE STORE

It is a long-established tradition in America. Every boy should have a girl. Those that don't are not men. Reaching a ripe age of eighteen means being independent and having a nice girl. Parents encourage children to find their first date before the 'D' day. The children either leave by themselves or are sometimes thrown out of the house after crossing the age of eighteen.

Spindle was aware of the culture. Back home children were treated differently. They could stay at the parents' house ad infinitum. The girls were to live with in-laws. Spindle was asked to find a girl for himself if he were to stay and work at the store. He sometimes walked out of the store during breaks to look for a girlfriend. Very soon, duty called and he ran in. Mr. Ahluwalia had girlfriends on the sly, so he said. He somehow managed to keep his girls away from the eyes of his mother. His mother too worked at another store. She wanted a traditional daughter-in-law and not some American. She raised the question to Mr. Ahluwalia, knowing that he was well settled and the ladder to success had no end. Mr. Ahluwalia brushed the question aside and replied,

"Ma, I have work to do. I have no time to have someone right now. I have to fulfil my dreams and have a store of my own. I don't want to work for anyone. Try to understand. When the time comes, I'll let you know."

His mother never dug in deep. She knew the value of having a son that was obedient and hard working. Besides she had another son that could be pursued.

The store was filled with people in the morning hours. At about eleven a grey-haired lady walked in with some children behind her. She had a warm smile. The group walked around the store and picked up things at random. Soon she stood at the cash counter with Spindle to assist her. The children, two in number, stood quietly behind her. She smiled and took everything the children had picked up for scanning at the counter,

"Haven't seen you before, are you new. These are my children and I would like you to scan these things and let me know."

"Madam, I am new. I will do the needful right away. Thank you and it's a beautiful day outside. Nice to meet you."

"It is beautiful, isn't it. Nice you meet you. I guess I'll be popping in again sometime. Thank you for your help, Bye."

"Pleasure is all mine, lady. You take care.

Spindle managed the cash register for a few hours. These were the peak hours when Anshu, Mr. Ahluwalia's elder brother too lend his hands. The rush was huge with the danger of pick pocketing the stuff left near the cash register. The Punjabis were hard on anyone caught cheating. The thieves were shunned from entering the store.

This lady with a grey hair came in the morning, sometimes on alternate days. Every time Spindle would greet her with,

"You look beautiful today. Store is all yours. Don't forget the cash register."

The lady blushed and her children dug deep into the little things they required for school. They stood at the cash register at the snap of the lady's fingers and she emptied her purse.

"Hi, I am Mrs. Turner. It's always a pleasure to see you, young man. Bye for now."

Mrs. Turner would often come to the store and shy away from Spindle's eyes knowing what he would say. Spindle loved the reaction of Mrs. Turner as she blushed away like a maiden.

FIFTEEN

THE FAT LADY

The biggest hurdle for Spindle was to find a place to stay. He had left Guest House Inns and Suites the day the boys left for home. From that time, he changed many places, most of them small hotels. Mr. Ahluwalia once suggested a guy that worked in another store. Spindle stayed there for a while until he found out that the guy was gay. Spindle then happened to run into this fat old lady that lived all alone. Mr. Ahluwalia and the owner had found out about the whereabouts of the lady. Her house was not far from the store Spindle worked at.

That fat lady, Mrs. Kimberly Watt, lived all alone in a big house. She welcomed Spindle and waited for him on a Sunday morning. Spindle carried all his belongings and rang the doorbell at about ten in the morning. A fat lady opened the door,

"You are the guest I'm expecting this morning, are you?"

"Yes madam, I'm the one."

"Please come in and bring your stuff in too. Gee you are a handsome hunk, aren't you?"

"Thank you, Mrs. Watt. Did I get your name right."

"That's right and I gather that you are from India."

"Yes, I am originally from India."

"Please come in. I have some coffee and cookies for you."

The two sat down in a beautiful living room. It was well lit with a from a side door that led to a back porch and a veranda. The room had wall hangings, spongy sofa cushions and a beautiful carpet of red and blue on the floor. Mrs. Watt was more than fifty years old with a deceased husband and two puppies. She lived all alone and was childless. The two puppies snuggled up against their new guest. Their tongues gauged the kind of person this new guest was and found him quite scrumptious. Mrs. Watt soon dumped Spindle's luggage in a small room and headed for her car. She took Spindle to a nearby Indian restaurant for some dosa. Living alone, Mrs. Watt longed for some company and Spindle was like a son to her. Indian food, especially south Indian, was quite popular on the west coast of America. It was light and not too spicy. Spindle liked his welcome and found a resting place, finally. He had become more of a gypsy, running around with rent in hand. There were the good ones and some very bad ones. He could never forget how he managed with a guy that turned out to be gay. Mrs. Watt was more traditional and belonged to the old school of survival. The only problem was her fixation to chocolate brownies that was killing her. She was already obese and knew how to prepare brownies and offer them to her guest. Spindle was fond of sweet but the sweet here had a different level. The pastries, brownies, donuts, apple pie, fudge were so high on sugar that it could saw down a healthy set of teeth in hours. Besides, American do not care for their oral health. Spindle did not want to decline an offer by Mrs. Watts. He just took a deep breath and let the brownie slide down his throat.

The room offered to Spindle had all the amenities that one could find in a hotel. It had a TV, fridge and a telephone. Spindle was addicted to smoking and every now and again wanted to take a smoke break. Mrs. Watts found out about the habit. She did not like it. A young man must invest his time in better things, she thought. However, she never stopped Spindle from smoking. She offered her veranda next to her living room as the space for him to smoke.

"Now, if you want to smoke, please step out and do it. I suggest you give up the habit. It could do great damage."

Spindle did smoke, but something dragged him away from the habit with each puff. He felt very embarrassed to smoke. He tried to hide to a vacant area when smoking. An addiction lives on false promises. But promise they do. The next day, or the next hour. But that never arrives. The habit is endless.

Mrs. Watt allowed Spindle to use her computer that had a gigantic screen. Spindle would often send emails to friends and family and search for a few things on the internet. Mrs. Watt washed Spindle's clothes in her washing machine which Spindle did not like. She often found matchsticks in his pocket, all wet, and would yell at Spindle, giving a warning to take action if repeated. Spindle could never give up smoking but tried not to leave matches in his pocket in the future.

It all ended one stormy night. Mrs. Watt in her room could not sleep all night. Spindle too lay on his bed, awake. The two lived through the night with eyes open. The next day when the storm was gone Mrs. Watt took a walk to Spindle's room. She was furious when she entered his room,

"What the heck. This is how you keep my room. You are so untidy. You have left the phone on the floor. What have you done to my bed; the bedsheet is sliding to the floor. I am afraid I will ask you to leave right away. Besides, I don't like smokers in my house. Get out and don't come back again."

Spindle quicky packed his bags and shifted to a nearby hotel with the help of Mr. Ahluwalia.

Many days later Spindle came to know that one of the dogs that Mrs. Watt owned had died.

SIXTEEN
THE FINAL SEE OFF

The time had come to leave. Spindle had completed three quarters in school. He was now eligible for a temporary work permit. He had spent many nights with Mr. Ahluwalia and his brother Anshu. They played cricket and football at night and roamed the streets in Mr. Ahluwalia's car. Mr. Ahluwalia was sad and didn't want to part with Spindle. Spindle felt the same and carried a world of experience on his shoulders. He could never find a permanent place to stay in the nine months he was at Mr. Ahluwalia's store. He shifted every three months; each time forced to leave and find a new tenant. Yet, he had never seen such beauty like California. The air was clean and the green like fresh colours in a canvas. Mr. Ahluwalia had been like a guide, a guru to Spindle. He gave him useful tips on living which Spindle carried the rest of his life. Mr. Ahluwalia consumed himself in smoking and drinking. He was on a suicide mission. He had decided never to get married. Spindle tried many times to kick the habit for he found it too embarrassing and corrupting a precious life. But Mr. Ahluwalia carried no qualms about burning his insides. He just wanted his elder brother to get settled while he perished in the process.

Spindle booked his plane tickets and bid adieu to Mr. Ahluwalia. He never came back. He returned to India after staying in the US for two more years.

"You'll never forget me.", were Mr. Ahluwalia's final words before parting.

Spindle and his time at the store were like sacred words in his book of life. He often went back to turn the pages and remember his wonderful time in America.

www.ingramcontent.com/pod-product-compliance
Lightning Source LLC
Chambersburg PA
CBHW031333130726
47988CB00007B/3114

FUTURE TECHNOLOGY TECHNOLOGY HOW INFLUENCES PASSENGERS PUBLIC TRANSPORT

CHOICE DECISION

JOHN LOK